Liquid Bones

Published in Tshwane, South Africa, by impepho
press in 2018
impephopress.co.za
ISBN 978-0-6399465-2-8

Edited by Vangile Gantsho
Cover art by Penelope Hunter
Cover and layout by Tanya Pretorius
Proofread by Tanya Pretorius, Abi Godsell,
   and Mjele Msimang

Print Production by [•] squareDot Media
Printing by Law Print

Earlier versions of some poems in this book have appeared
in the following websites, literary journals and anthologies:
"uNongqawuse and the New People": *The Atlanta Review*, 2018;
"hold": *Illuminations*, 2017; "for the guns", *Astra*, 2016

Liquid Bones
Sarah Godsell

"I'm a gathering of everybody and nobody, of everything and nothing. Is there anyone else you'd like to invite? Everyone's invited."
Arundhati Roy – *The Ministry of Utmost Happiness*

Table of Contents

a dream of a world we can change

there is no green here

our voices made wings

that step, that note

Alone

on the wings of our birds

a dream of a world we can change

hold[1]

---

1   this country of blood

     where if I spit
     your blood comes out my mouth

     this blood
     that not even the mountains can hold

     this country   made of singing

wizard. witch. sage.

I am part wizard
part witch
part sage

part humble
part hubris

part bookshelf
part wine rack

part archive
part stage

part classroom
part hand-in-hand sweat.

Part hidden in footsteps
collecting the imprints.

Part standing on beach
commanding the waves.

Part heart of the march
part inch above head

part sleep
part death
part umbilical cord

part past
part hope

Part you'll-never-believe-me.
Part challenge me, I'll swallow you.
Part hold me, I'm hurting.
Part super-human.

Part dancing
Part weeping
Part wizard. Part witch. Part sage

Stones, dancing

I kissed you.   I could feel songs
                     in your mouth

like crickets.

We touched fingers.   Webs grew between,
all my drought caught in them.

                     We sat in front of

your gran's bookshelf,
dust whispering into our skin:

baptismal roots,   my godmother in that
photo,
                  90s faded

your tongue wrapping around phonemes
                  holding people together
                  unaware

your fragments   dream maps
for new worlds.

Our teeth bumped.
               Awkward,
recalled to here, now.

Our dreams were always
              crashing stones
              dancing,

I should have known then that the dance would
turn them to dust.

Reach you
for Natasha

I am full of tears today

enough to quench Joburg's trees,
turn me into a thunderstorm,
let my fire out in lightning.
turn to an ocean   a whirlwind   a cyclone
screaming across the seas   to you.

When I am done weeping
                    when I reach you
                                        I will not be
                                        so very full
                                        of tears.

Marry me on Tuesday

Marry me on Tuesday
or don't marry me
at all.

Marry me on Tuesday,   under the jacaranda
                                                      tree

I will wear my Cookie Monster t-shirt
       you
will wear your rings.

Marry me on Tuesday.
Or don't marry me at all.

We have this moment.
We had.

Or we don't
at all.

tiny flying

there are smears of dead mosquitoes on my ceiling
the other night I had a killing frenzy
smack
smacking them
dead
doing the on-the-bed dance
chasing after tiny flyings
I remember my mom doing this
my baby sister was in the middle bunk
I was on top
my mom on the floor
reading to us
falling asleep
she would spring up
smack
smacking them
dead
smears of blood on the wall
the move was so sudden we would jump
laugh
my mom doing the silly
on-the-bed dance
chasing after tiny flyings
hand hitting the ceiling
smack
smacking them
dead
squashing tiny monsters

The PebbleMoon Song

Walking one night
a pebble slipped inside my shoe

Slowing down
I watched the moon move
matching my hobbling to her flow

I learnt to sing
that night
swapping speed for song

I sewed this secret into the sole of my foot
kissed the stone

I will never walk as fast again.
I will never forget to sing.

there is no green here

I am so busy
sweeping
the dead flies
from the floor
that I have
 no time to
deal with
the body
attracting
the flies
in the corner

mimosa
> *For Vangile*

I must speak to you about the mimosa flowers. At night, in my safe, square bed, in my safe, square house, I read about 1856 and 1857 in Xhosaland. British Kaffraria, Transkei, Ciskei, the Eastern Cape. Where the stars are God's special gift.

(her prayer,
you said.)

where you held my hand, let me in
laughed as I tucked my skirt into my panties,
danced in your river.

What words are used for "frontier" wars?   loss   loss   loss. Magic, Mlanjeni. Muthi against bullets has never worked. Not then. Not in Marikana. I must   speak to you about lungsickness that collapsed on constant grabbing of the land thieves, that collapsed on drought. uNongqawuse. Prophet. Weaving Words of Worlds without Whites. Her words were a smoking dream bridge. The red coats pushed your people to edge of chasm anyway. Nothing   to   do   but   Jump
wait for New People   in the fall

or turn around,
slip into thin lips of colonists,
into wage labour spelt like slavery.

uNongqawuse spoke of relief, restored autonomy, resistance against cold english steel. Her words called for a New World. For New to be Made all had to be Burnt. Slaughtered. Everything left ready for New People.   Who would not come. What came was sssstarvation. Year after year, after year, after hundreds of thousands,   dead. The efficient thin lips did everything. Nothing. Took only those fleeing, Hunger at their Heels. Signed them into slavery that was spelt wage labour. They signed. Trying to twist the letters into anything but hunger.
It was this moment that destroyed   a   way of life

(the thin lips smiled)
amaGcaleka, amaMpondo, amaNdlambe, amaThembu. Didn't
Destroy. Because you are here. You are Here. Descendant of
survivors. I am here. Thin-lipped.   Bloodlines.

                              you have held me in your hand.
               I still have not been able to speak to you about
                                  the mimosa flowers:
people   starving. Queenstown residents   "care society" for
people   dying shadows on roads.

one said
when the starving
shadows slipped in all they
smelt of was hunger   and the mimosa tree.

Mimosa bark. The only thing left to eat in a landscape sacrificed
to call the New People. Who would not come. Landscape
sucked up by thin-lipped smiles. Thin lipped governor only
allowed help for those already dying. Only if, as soon as they
could stand, they were signed over into the colony, as labour.
They smelt of mimosa and starvation.

                    cruel sweet scent

Now, in Johannesburg, I drive into mimosa street, pass
mimosa school. Starving Shadows.

How will we speak of the scent
of the mimosa
 1856   1857

                                        cruel
                                        sweet
                                        scent

           we speak in impepho smoke and everything between the lines
                and committing committing committing

15

Nongqawuse and the New People

What do I wear on Heritage Day?

map of stolen land
veil of screams

dark red lipstick:
caked centuries of rape

high-heeled shoes
made of bones
of slaves

rings of border wars
indentured labour

arm ornaments
beaded delicately
in languages lost

necklaces of bullets
collected from bodies

hair tied with rainbows
that double as nooses.

I will wear nothing.
Not even words.
I will sit.
Wait for uNongqawuse
and the New People
to rise from the soil.

Visiting Hours

Dear   former   President   Thabo   Mbeki,
There is a 14 year old in ICU at the clinic down the road.
The visiting hours are: 11-12,   3-4,   7-8

Will you go and see her?

She has been unconscious for 5 days now. Her   brain
keeps seizing. They don't know when she will wake up
or how or why. They do not speak of the disease in her
blood.

Dear   former President   Thabo Mbeki
two weeks ago we were celebrating her 14th birthday.
She was blowing out candles on an ice   cream   cake
wrapped in shy-bold 14 year old singing   as her friends
(young.brave.growing) shy   awkward, self-assured
future facing   looked with her   into   next   year.
The visiting hours are: 11-12,   3-4,   7-8

Will you go and see her?

As I sit next to her   whispering that she   can   go on
all the adventures she needs   in the dark
in those world's we cannot   see   or   taste
whispering   to her   not to go to close to the sun
as her temperature rises   whispering   to her
not to run so much   when her heart rate spikes

As I sit here, her mom (she has two. They are transparent,
shivering like butterfly wings   fragile in their   fear
desperation) takes out the bottles containing   ARVs
we cannot speak those letters either, they are down on
the charts as "OWN MEDICINE". Nurse smiles gently
She has already prepared them. Her hands hold silence

Here, in this hospital   in South Africa, we cannot
speak the letters. We cannot breathe   ARVS   I wonder
how   can this not affect this   14 year old
silent   sweating   with   super hero   hair

if answers from doctors have gotten   lost in the
silence   because no one is holding her mothers' hands
explaining   what is happening   in their daughter's
brain. She is just left   hanging.   In limbo.
Wrapped in the silence. All of us   standing outside
our noses pressed against the silence: Willing her out
Willing her up.   Willing her 14 year old   into
her   15 year old   into her   35 year old

But, I am asking, former   President Thabo Mbeki
if you will go and see her, because,   14   years   ago
a mother gave birth to a child.   A mother who was
not given Nevirapine   gave birth   to this child

Surely   we knew then?   About the Nevirapine?
That this 14 year old could be   dancing   now   not
silent   sweating   in the dark

DearFormerPresidentThaboMbeki   the visiting
hours are 11–12,   3-4,   7-8.   Will you go and see her?[2]

---

2   *If she dies, will you come to her funeral?*

I love you

I love you
Which means
I hate you
Which means
You're cruel and destroying me
Which   I will never forgive you
     means I cannot let go of you
Which means please leave
Which means don't let   go
Which means   let me go
            I don't love you anymore

Which means
I love you

For the Guns

The guns crawl out of themselves
this night

They leave their metal carcasses
The student struggles out of his coat
as the policemen wrestle him

He escapes

black

Into the night

The police are left
with the ghost of the coat
still asking them

what did I do?

The guns hear
They crawl out of themselves
leaving the police with their metal carcasses

They crawl into the throat
of the student

into her rage, into her fear
This is what they are used to eating

Instead they find themselves
abandoned even by her

The guns weep
because the policemen   will   not.
                       (can)

Caught in the web of the question
she keeps asking the policemen

standing there with the metal carcasses of the guns:

How can you not see that you are killing your child?[3]

3   *UJ Night Vigil, 15 November 2015.*

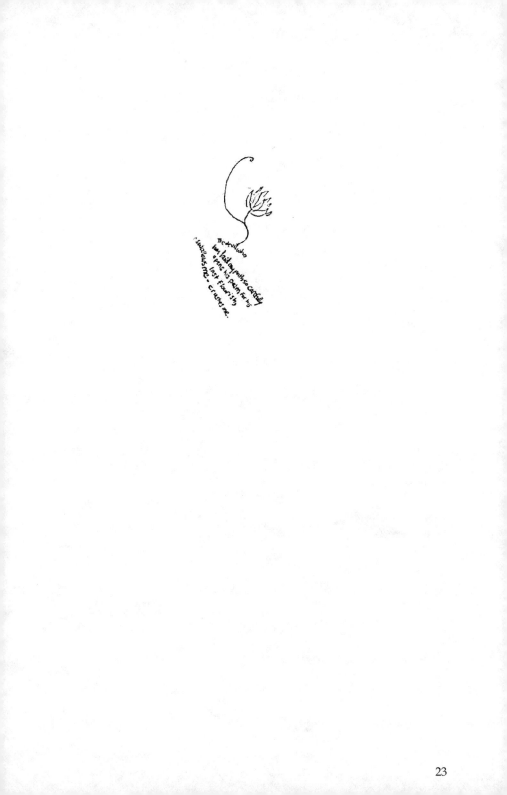

The cruel lover
had laid me, palm so carefully
against his palm for his
scandalous last flourish
scandalous me... crushed me.

our voices made wings

the spiders under my skin are trying to escape
They have smelt the sun
They are tired of hiding in my blood

I wonder
what will happen
when they are set free?

Sylvia

"I am terrified by this dark thing
That sleeps in me" Elm by Sylvia Plath

I sit here in my earth   your face
cupped in my hand
You   in your   Pink Wool Dress,
years distant
already star marked   you did not yet
Speak of the marks of your   Panther
          haunting   hunting you
Your Panther   my Bear
          living death   in shadows

                                                              but

I know I will not die like that.
          like you.
                              [we no longer use gas ovens
                                        I imagine my death more elegant
                              cannot imagine   leaving a child
                                                  maybe just cannot imagine
                                        mother to anything blood-like]

I sleep Curled in it. Warm
Claws on my breasts, my Bear turns into
My   Elephant, and tendrils,
curling in my sleep.
                              I dream of
love not soured, Sylvia,
my tears not matching your bright
but my salt on Your [4]   cheek as I lick it.
Your flesh Warm
Through Ocean and Oven

---

4   *(clown-like, happiest on your hands) You're*   *Sylvia Plath*

bored of Eternity, and yes, you are Vertical, a straight

silver strand of death   hope   longing

in my hand.

"I've eaten a bag of green apples,
Boarded the train there's no getting off." Metaphors   Sylvia Plath

Trophy[5]

                    THERE HAVE BEEN OTHERS
                         ALWAYS OTHERS

                    DID HE FEEL LIKE THIS?
                           DO THEY
                    ALWAYS FEEL LIKE THIS?

I cut his penis off

think about swallowing it

                    THERE ARE OTHER WEAPONS
                         ALWAYS OTHERS

I hand it to him

Suggest he mount in on the wall
to remind him
of the shadows he has set in stone.

                                        ALWAYS

                                        OTHERS

                                        OTHERS

                                        OTHERS

---

5   *To the man who raped my best friend.*

Wonder.[6]

I have visions

*In three years he will feel himself powerful and impotent enough
to rape you*

but
because I have visions
and you are made of birds and snakes,
because I can see the world in your throat when
you laugh

I will not allow that

MY SISTER'S FRIEND. MY SISTER.   ME.
ALWAYS OTHERS.

somehow

You protect your threeyearold daughter
you and her
wings and ribs-as-feet

somehow

you have kept your wonder.
That is wonder enough for me.

---

6   *Others.*   *Always.*   *Others.*

Forget the Ground[7]

I want to carve a stone for you
with a small door
for you to hide in
when you are exhausted
the world pulling on every appendage,
climbing up your tears,
into your eyes
to pick through your mind
mining diamonds   rushing them away from you
to shine in the sun.

The stone is temperature flexible:
warm, in your chest, when your fear is cold,
cool when your anger is burning.
It speaks your languages
so no one else can claim it   or you.
It reminds you:

   You are everything.

You deserve rest.
You deserve space.
You deserve holding where you don't have to be brave.
You deserve lightness.
You deserve gentle dark.
You deserve softness where you do not have to think
      who to thank.
You deserve to explore without having to hold.
You deserve love without having to speak.
You deserve wings where you do not have to
fear what will happen to the ground when you   fly.

---

7   *For BeautifulBraves. For Holders. Dreamers. Who makes oceans. Volcanoes.*
   Who must rest.

breathe not

light filters through water

everything is dilute

breath hardly moves

it would cost nothing to breathe less

to breathe not

head breaks surface

salt fills my lungs

I crawl onto the beach

friends sit   watching

legs spread   salt in all   wounds

pass the wine   pass the weed   pass the vodka

pass the sadomasochism books   the poemtrees

Plant our feet.

If any of us choose to breathe less

to breathe   not

we will make sure it is not a nothing choice

the choice to leave will be a fight:

if you choose that hard

we will trace you in the sky

with our tongues

in the night.

Fireheads

For Larissa

i climb inside your coffin. lie next to you. cheek on your
chest. i hold your heart. feel it beating. i kiss you warm. feel
your fingers begin to move as they are watered by my tear-
springs on your chest. you wake, hold me weeping, tell me
this is just a bad dream. we sit in your coffin as if in a bath: feet
to feet. we speak of growing up. of trying to put our hearts in
men   watching them shattered   shattered again. we
laugh at first loves, remember the wildness with which we ran.
we trip, of course. i soothe you with rhymes about sticks and
stones. you remind me it was words that broke you.

i don't look at your skeleton. the holes left by the times he
left you for me. i match my bones to yours: similar holes. me
for you. me, breathing. we grow sombre at last loves, death
strung between us. he places us carefully each at one end of
the rope. we look down and pull. he sits on the sidelines,
waiting to see which of our fire-haired heads bows first. when
i see that death lies in the middle of that rope
i scream   so loud   it leaves   him paralysed. i drop
the rope   run to you   hold your wrists in my hands   feel your
pulse   shocked into the silence of 'almost' i breathe out a
bridge in front of us lead us together into starcountry two fire-
heads turning away from death.

I climb out of your coffin.
Too heavy for him to carry
Both of us

Choosing him to
carry your body. Prize and punishment.

I will not die like this.
I weep. Write you alive.

Mark a dark spot in my heart
for conversations we should have had.

Build Us New Cities[8]

"I am made of fire
The sun is my father
I have 276 and 241 and 263 mothers

I was born with
a tamed terror in me

My nightmares weave spiderwebs
stronger than states

Earthworms of fire tunnel through my chest
I have never tried to escape them

When I set them free
they will build us new cities
of fire and sun

Founded on heartbeats of girl-mothers
nightmares of warghost fathers
we no longer run from."

---

8   *Instructions for reading: find a shell, raise it to your ear, listen to Titilope Sonuga's*
    Hide and Seek:

    " it must mean those children are still asleep
    they are safe in their beds
    their dreams a kaleidoscope of color"

Against the storm

Every jacaranda
against every stormy sky
is heart
against hope.

Parts stubbornly refusing
to be swallowed by whole.
Whole gently licking and
holding parts.

Is cycle reminding us of where we were.
Where we are.
Where we will never be again.

Who will always be gone   ?
How will they always be with you   ?

Is shutting your eyes to the fall.
Finding the gentle cushions of wind
in the storm.[9]

---

9   *this country made of singing*

Those of us
With liquid bones that sing
With voices of birds whose wings... there
If we are not lucky   we do not find
step, that note, our hands do not find each...
Pain is better only
The path just grows. Dark grows thicker
Mud creeps up our legs. We cannot move   come
Our voices swallowed by the devil's laughter   Me alone
No hope
In pain; Unable. With liquid bones   they whisper you
The trees suggest it first   here; have no place here
The sky will try and sing me home, if she sees me.
but the trees enclose me, & kills laughter

that step, that note

i wonder how many skin cells are in my bed

if they could make a whole person

if they could make a person, maybe

that I actually want in my bed with me.

Burning Bones
   for Wopko Jensma, and those on the bus

You disappeared in
         the fire

40 years later you
         open your mouth

fire spews out

you burn our eyebrows
off
         turn our clothes to ash

burn off the skin we tent ourselves in

until we are just
              bones

a collection of skeletons
open to the breeze of bullets
your words blow through us

Verona

We watched opera in Verona
over 10 years ago.
I don't remember which opera
Aida, maybe?

All our childhood
caught in one breath,
you were around me, always,
in my name   inside my first
deciphering of words
out of stubbornness   because you could.

We learnt together.
My chin-forward,
able to adventure
because of your fragilestrong.
We stood against the wind.

That night Verona's arena
held us together, basket of stars, voice,
so close we didn't need to hold hands.

Over 10 years ago.[10]

I miss you

---

10 *The opera was la traviata. I found the songbook. Wikipedia translates it as "fallen
woman". Rising Falling Sinking Flying. I smile. You are turning into flowers.*

Beach Lullaby[11]

I am learning to let go of you

      to uncurl my hands from the shells of you
      that I have already crushed
      rain is washing
      fragments of you

from   my clenched fingers

      all I have left are cuts
      from shells
      in my hand

memory of rock pools we explored

      we dug our holes
      on the beach
      comforted, still child-excited

our hands met in the middle.

              You were always looking   out

            to a star
        to the mist on the sea
      a lullaby I could never hear

---

11 *Lost*

I hate the wind.   The song I cannot hear.   I hate that
I have lost you.

I am learning to let go
of you
finding small animals
to lick the blood of us left on my hands

                I hope
your   crushed   shells   might   catch the wind

my sweat   your sand
together
in some sweeping song

Mercury to Gold

I remember
being small, sick,
feverburning.

I dropped a thermometer from my mouth. It
shattered on the tiled floor.

I watched, amazed
as tiny mercury bubbles rushed around my feet:
small silver creatures, faster than my fingers could follow.

My parents put me on a chair,
told me to keep my feet up:
those silver creatures are poisonous!

I watched,
eyes feverbright
as my parents took off their gold wedding rings
to coax the mercury-animals
Together
into a teaspoon.

I have never known what they did with that poison.

Narina Trogon

You are nothing
Just   Gone

planting in me
a fear of death
    impractical for someone
so   suicidal

I am not afraid of the pain
I am not even afraid for me
I am afraid of the nothing

the world is peopled with someones who can
just disappear.

except you don't.   Disappear.

Flowers die quickly
in my garden.

You,   rare redgreen bird,   are still here.
In my head.

ode to leaving

heartbreak feels
like icewater down your spine

realising you swallowed a fly

like you ate too much ice-cream
and you won't feel better
until you throw up

sometimes. it feels like
your legs giving up on your brain
                              walking off without you.

sometimes. you have to set your sights on a sunset
and leave.

Clowns
L'Aquila, Italy

They came in rainbow squeaks
trickling in drips
from all over the country.

They came in trains
their coloured wigs bouncing
as they sat in silence
waiting to arrive.

They came in cars
squeaky shoes overrevving accelerators
as they drove, not talking, purposeful

They came from the top, bottom, middle
of the country
answering a call
spread through the shock waves

They came
to a small town outside Rome
that sat wringing its hands
thick with grief

No one speaks as they sift through the rubble

The clowns arrive, cartwheel in
smiles ready
painted in technicolour
to ease the razor edges of a new day

They spin in,
take people's hands, dance
spray water out of plastic flowers
washing the taste of death with custard pies
gently, gently, helping to clear the rubble

For an hour

another

one more.

friendship[12]

She tries to stand on the edge of her.
To throw ropes of flowers down the sides of
the pit to her,   comfort   way out, as
she sings of her own death. Voice
crumbling into the darkness.

She, on the edge, hears the singing from the deep. Stays
teetering. Peering. Singing fades. From the edge
she calls   calls. Hears nothing.

She adjusts her ropes, climbs
  down, confident of
ropes'   strength. Confident of not losing   light.
Brazen in mission.

Halfway down, Climber hears a   voice
from the outside. She had climbed up   out.   Safe.
Was drinking tea with their friends.
Tea-drinker laughs at the panic. The tangle of ropes.

---

12 *harnesses and other safety protocols are not often considered for these journeys*

That her friend had climbed down to her.
why didn't you trust me?   her eyes flashed.

Poured tea onto Climber.
Down the hole. Down her friend's cheeks
like tears. Halfway up. Halfway down.

Lost in her dark.

Bougainvillea

Bright pink bougainvillea paint my city
Peacocking, rivalling jacaranda's purple
Falling down vines, tumble over
your metal gate. Their bold chaos needs
something to climb, something to hold
the all-fall-down stumbling

Me, crumpling like the creeper,
around, through, over you

I keep your metal gate in my mind:
padlock's precise boundaries

You inside
Me outside

I wonder if I can change myself
to metal gate
from crawling bougainvillea?

Standing.
Not crumbling.
In the all-fall-down.

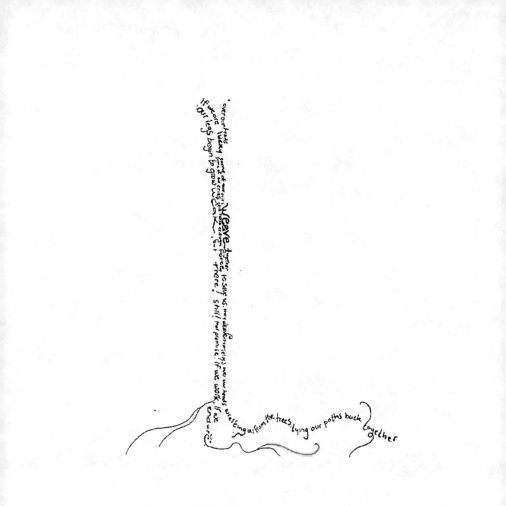

our own roots, growing at our will... weave together to stop us, my wandering rivers... never our roots, wrestling us from the trees, tying our paths back together

If not our lucky gods at crisis point, enough force, to stay there, still my promise, if we work, if we end... There

our legs begin to grow together... still

53

Alone

ice bones creak softly
summoning season change
my fingers snap on your cheek
before your blood can warm me

Lonely for nothing

I am lonely for nothing
I am lonely for a revolution
I am lonely for a world that will not come

I am lonely for a lover
I am lonely for love
I am lonely for a touch that will destroy me

I am lonely for an echo
I am lonely for a sound I know
I am lonely for a chasm to throw my echo into

I am lonely for my best friend
I am lonely for a hand in my chest
I am lonely for a dream that exists only as ghost

I am lonely for comrades
I am lonely for lovers
I am lonely for an everyday that does not hurt

I am lonely for dark
I am lonely for death
I am lonely for a piece of a peace of a sunset

In her flight

A spotted eagle-owl visited me last night
while I was gathering many corners of a triangle

She hooted at me
looking out of place

I opened the door to let her in
she stayed outside
safe
watching me

I collected my fingers
phoned you,
told you about the owl

                                        what does she want?
you asked. Said
you felt her in the owl.

found   in her flight
where she had flown, taken the jump off the chair

                        found possibility of movement
where her feet had been treading air

In her hoot, you heard her voice
her broken neck   swallowing her goodbye

                        Hello
you said to the owl
237 kilometres away

I love you

you said to the owl   through me

I turned the phone away
all my heartpieces   escaping

new waves of her   of hurt

                                                                I love you.

I said

She flew.   Outside.   Away.   Where it is safe.

Flowers in the window

I have a place where my panes of glass
have been worn thin
By wings beating
By morning breath blown
Rubbed

I realise
the journey never fills the
space behind these panes

the flowers I have been hoping for

inside my windows

will never grow

Or if they do they will die
before and around me

I will keep tracing
messages to no-one
in my breath
on my panes

death and my hand

i sprayed a black widow's nest
She was poised,
spinning her nest mildly.

Small amounts of poison,
in a nest, in a garden.

She did nothing.

wish i could have invited her
into my hands
felt her web,
her life
her poison
on my fingers

coals

Basket protected me from Monsters. Taught me. Shouted
 when i was careless with toys   time   flames.
When i missed hungry pockets of thunder Basket always
saw. Wide-eyed.   In joy.   In fear.
With me.

Held pain in our palms, imagined into monsters we
invented. Controlled. Never-almost.
Carved with blood on our skin sung
with teenage angst: manageable thunderstorms.
With me.

Basket left me. Found a way out
like a cat
burned as a witch.

                 Basket set fire to herself.

            I can understand your need to leave. Your fleeing
            feet needed the burning coals to run from. I have
            anger in spurts. Burn wounds. Old bone breaks
            that ache when it's sunny. A missing limb I keep
                    forgetting is   gone as   I
                 turn wide-eyed   in fear   in joy

to empty air.

grief finds flight

There is no time for grief
in this fight

but she wells up

She grows into something:
through our bodies
finds flight

What will she become?

Where will her feathers,

as they grow into our arms,

take us?

Or she will turn monster. Plughole sucking us in. All attempts
to avoid, Pompei-like, leave us atrophied.

I avoid those bodies in Pompei. I pivot.
Turn away from myself.

Mirror. Reflection.

Sharp curves of feather quills. Pain in my skin. When I can face
myself again. I will have wings.

on the wings of our birds

we speak blood,   bodies
death   blood
we   speak   lifeblood
every month growthblood
swelling   in aches
reminding us of   space
the   moon   reserves
to nurture us in her shape

no such thing as grown-up
for our daughters, if we have them

There is a wry smile on my lips
as I watch my friends turn 30.
Proudly. In many constellations.

I saunter towards that mark,
not particularly interested in
the honeycombs behind me.

Not concerned with the pools
that will mirror gravity, ahead

Feeling that this decade will be
more mine
than the previous ones.

> Mark this survival.
> Weeping. Blood. Dancing.

> Make each
> day more our own.

> Owning our lonely.

> Somewhere there are magic wands.
> Here there is wine.
> And song.

Almost morning

I am thinking about you.
Imagining my head on your breast

if I am honest,
I am imagining your nipple in my mouth
the weight of your breasts in my hands
our thighs, crossing over, under, each other
tangled

I am imagining kissing you
sitting face-to-face
our bodies touching.

How strange, how good it feels
to press my breasts to yours.
How your hair smells,
as I pull your head to mine

your breath in my ear
not moaning
Your noises dance more beautifully
than that

A strange, transparent, bird-animal,
singing, in the
inbetween light
of the almost morning

I am imagining how my body responds to yours
before my head does
how I am caught, surprised,
pulled behind the waves of pleasure
how I hold your curves gentle,

body curves, hair curves
tracing the freckles on your shoulder

I would like to kiss you again

bed spreads
For Danai and her Mikha

Now, body
spread across my bed
She takes up so much more space
Look how small she once was,
my baby

catching the fire in the skin
serious   dance-face
tears   to salt our gardens

Now-bodies
spread across our heads
Look how tall we are, my babies.

Home Song

Go well.
with shells in your hair,
wings on your ankle bones.

Go with snake-familiars in
your belly,
calligraphy on your map.

Go well
with all the tears shed for you
making waves for you to ride,
laughing.

Go with no broken bones
or bruises on your body
or your heart.
Go with desert flowers
cacti
holding your hands, their needles
bending soft for you, under your fingers.

Go well.
Go with no dis ease.
Go carried on carpets of autumn leaves,
go with laughter calling,   calling,   calling
You Home.

Guerrilla: BeautifulBraves of 2015[13]

The guerrillas are
Drawing breath
Choosing weapons
Loving each other up
Testing skin thickness, weather resistance
Holding the songs in their throats
Getting ready for next year

---

13 *a member of a small independent group taking part in irregular fighting, typically against larger regular forces #feesmustfall*

Liquid Bones

The devil has gone neoliberal.
He has won over the warlords.
He is coming after each of us.

II

His path is laid s l o w l y.
He plants SunFlowers on our paths
finds our favourite colours,
sells us a dream   of a world we can change,

if we work hard enough.
Or,   we can, at least, be happy. If we work.

He draws us each onto our own path.
We can no longer hold hands.
We do not notice. We are too busy working. Hard.
There is a promise at the end.

III

     We walk. The flowers start to wilt, then die.
   We push forward.
The promise is still there!
   If we endure.

IV

The path grows.
   The dark grows thicker.
      there is

no   green   here

  we grow
desperate. Call out: someone!
      anyone?

Our legs grow weak, but   there!
    Still!   That promise!
        If we work.
        If we endure.

V

If we are   lucky

some of our cries weave together
some of our cries still have enough force
    to save us
they weave themselves over our heads
wresting us from the trees
tying our paths back together

        We   grasp   each other
        This is a   battle
        We cannot stop screaming.

VI

Our cries: wing feathers
over   our   heads
a bird beating her wings in the devil's face:

He must retreat
He must retreat

Our voices are wings strong enough to save us.
If we are lucky.
we are drenched in the pain
                    still walking.
dressing each-others wounds
        planting flowers in them.

If we are not lucky
we do not find that step, that note,
our hands do not find each other,
the path just grows.
Dark grows thicker
Mud creeps up our legs
We cannot move.
Our voices swallowed by the devil's laughter.
There is only me. Alone.
With liquid bones. No hope. No choice.

VII

The trees suggest it first.
They whisper:[14]

---

14 *You have no place here*

VIII

The sky will try and sing me hope! If she sees me.
but   the trees enclose me,
the devil's laughter swallows me.

the devil who has laid my path so carefully
opens his palm for his last flourish,
crushes   me,
laughing.

IX

The devil has gone neoliberal.
He has won the   warlords
filled the   sky with drones
licked the   bank   notes
infiltrated   the   unions[15]

15 *but he will not win the sky.*

X

We, liquid bones, sing.
With voices of birds,
voices who have found each other,

sending swarms of birds to wrest
the ones he grabs from his fists

we rescue the still warm bodies[16]
    draw them with us into the sky
    their souls melting into the songs of our
    liquid bones

The Devil has only a moment of triumph.

---

16 WE ARE NEVER ALONE

Breath crystallizes.

   in out in.

      nothing to be done.

         in this frozen soil hides

            the sun.

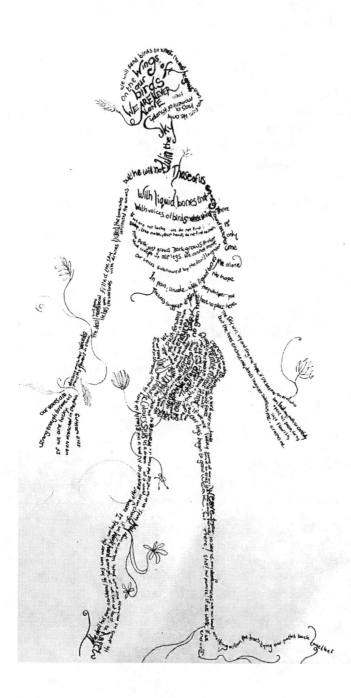

83

Acknowledgements

This second book has been birthed in shards and stones, in much less fertile soil. More blood but also more green. I was closer to death but pulled myself away from it harder; I had forests of hands to help me as I pulled. The following names leave out many who have also saved my life:

Vangile. You are in my poems and spirit and hope. In my building and tears. In my seaweed sky and my bones. We have many countries and poems and stories to travel together, still. I am grateful, grateful, grateful.

Lerato. You are a special castle. Built with love and hurt in every brick. You have so many people fighting for your life – never forget the direction and the song you choose are yours.

Busisiwe. I used to see you shapeshift from cloud to glass to tree root. Now, when you solidify, it is into a shape that is nothing we have seen in this world yet. I am excited for all of your dimensions.

Thandokuhle. You taught me brave and gnashing teeth and never-lose-your-voice when I met you. You have maintained that bravery in notes that melt into fragile, into abandon, into laughter.

Natasha. I dreamt once you taught me to box. You have taught me motherhood as a dimension, friendship as a journey, minds as caves we sometimes find ourselves underwater in. I love you in shades of cactus and bitter-aloe as well as comfort food. I am forever grateful for Taariq. Morning Star.

Talya. We have shared different forms of emotions, of handheart holding. We share clumsy. We share skin. I don't know if you know I look to you for an example of brave. I appreciate your honesty and loyalty and gentle. I love you in falling.

Danai. The way you hold space, with generosity and fire breathe. Watching you love in dimensions. Learn healing. Heal.

Mikha. For the poem in your heart and the fire in your skin.

Dianne. For the brave that never stops burning in your chest.

Penny. For new journeys on canvas and through caves.

Megan. We are losing and finding each other. I love you in the space and absence, in your presence and the green light you glow with. We are intertwined, together, or apart. We have the beach, always. I am held by your brave and by your commitment. I love you. I love you. I love you.

Abi. Small sister, in hope and spreadsheets. Building cities, and new structures, and imagining new worlds. I wish for you calming waves each night. I wish for you holding. I love you in and out of the maps you are making.

Mpho. Darling, I hope one day we can find a world that is not a seesaw, to sit and laugh. And play. Know that I am constantly proud of you.

Vanessa. Again, I am alive because of the space we have held.

impepho press. A catapult journey of building and healing that asks of us more than we think we can and gives us back more than we can expect to hold. I am humbled and excited for the future.

Mjele. Learning to love you, holds me soft and hard when I need, teaches me vibrant, pastel, smoke, history and song, and bones. How Up is also forward, is also holding, also rest, also laughter, also loss.

Gillian and Bobby. You teach brave companionship, and constant learning. You teach not to be afraid of battling with dirt under nails. You teach the importance of, voice, of books, and integrity, and of bravery in exhaustion. Of admitting and owning and never accepting hopelessness. You teach responsibility, of coming back, and of how we must continue to believe in possibilities. We are working through our pasts towards futures.

Hall. Godsell. Carlisle. Oates. Evertt. Colijn. Bloodlines. Lost Ones. I am learning you.

impepho
press

TITLES

feeling & ugly by danai mupotsa

Surviving Loss by Busisiwe Mahlangu

red cotton by vangile gantsho

Printed in the United States
By Bookmasters